WHAT DOES THE BIBLE REALLY SAY ABOUT DOMESTIC VIOLENCE?

WHAT DOES THE BIBLE REALLY SAY ABOUT DOMESTIC VIOLENCE?

DR. LéNETTA BANKS

The LeNetta Banks Group, LLC

Published by The LeNetta Banks Group, LLC
P.O. Box 241802
Montgomery, AL 36124
drbanks@lenettabanks.com
1-844-7-DRBANKS

Special discounts are available on quantity purchases by corporations, associations, educators and others. For details, contact The LeNetta Banks Group, LLC at the above listed address.
U.S. trade bookstores and wholesalers: Please contact The Lenetta Banks Group, LLC at the following email address: drbanks@lenettabanks.com.

ISBN: 978-1-518-60031-9

Typesetting services by BOOKOW.COM

I dedicate this book in loving memory of my mother, role model and hero in the field of human service, Mrs. Dolly Rebecca Banks.

FOREWORD

Domestic abuse is a more frequent and serious issue than most realize. Things you should know:
- Every nine seconds in the U.S. a woman is assaulted or beaten.
- Domestic violence is the leading cause of injury to women—more than car accidents, muggings, and rapes combined.
- Studies suggest that up to ten million children witness some form of domestic violence annually.
- Everyday in the U.S., more than three women are murdered by their husbands or boyfriends.
- Ninety-two percent of women surveyed listed reducing domestic violence and sexual assault as their top concern.
- Men who, as children, witnessed their parents' domestic violence were twice as likely to abuse their own wives than sons of non-violent parents.

LéNetta Banks, a domestic abuse survivor, becomes a Moses to captive women through the pages of this book. She shows women the way to the Promised Land of freedom from abuse and the path to wholeness and healing. This is not just an ordinary book on domestic abuse but a look at what God's word says about the topic, and rightfully so. There has been no religious book throughout history more kind to women than the Bible. It was written in a day where Greco-Roman Culture:
- Forbade girls from going to school or speaking in public
- Did not allow women to leave the house without a male with them
- Taught men to keep their wives locked up
- Treated women as slaves
- Considered women as inferior to men

Jesus taught things like:

"Husbands, love your wives, just as Christ loved the church." And He added, "He who loves his wife loves himself."

Additionally, Jesus treated all women with great respect, from the women at the well to Mary and Martha. In What does the Bible Really Say About Domestic Violence?, LéNetta Banks decrees and declares over readers:

"...Woman, thou art loosed from thine infirmity..." Luke 13:12

You may not think of domestic abuse as an infirmity, but it traps, confines and binds many in the same manner as physical infirmity. This book is the balm that will cause many to find relief. Thank you, LéNetta, for such a masterpiece.

Before you embark into the pages of this book, I want to pray for you. Whether you are a victim of domestic abuse, a survivor of domestic abuse or one seeking knowledge to help others, I pray that:

God would grant clarity and boldness to you as you read this book. May courage arise and fear dissipate. May The Great Lord show you who you really are in His eyes (fearfully and wonderfully made).

If you have been a victim of domestic abuse, may the mental and emotional scars that mistreatment has left you be healed. May you forgive your abusers and yourself. May you rise above the ashes of broken promises of love that were lies. May God grant you the courage to love again, believe again, trust again and feel again. May the controlling spirits that have dominated your relationships be broken.

Let Grace be the wind beneath your wings. Rest in the redemptive power of God's love and His ability to restore your soul. Lastly, remember that your value is not determined by who you were but by the Great I AM!!

Bishop Kyle Searcy
Presiding Bishop,
Fresh Anointing House of Worship
Montgomery, AL
www.kylesearcy.com

"LéNetta, when my daughter heard you speak out on domestic violence on the Capitol steps with the Governor and First Lady, you really changed her life. You were not the stereotype; you were a poised and professional woman who also survived. She finally saw herself and decided to leave her abuser."

This testimony is at the heart of LéNetta Banks' passion for people.

Dr. LéNetta Banks is a domestic violence awareness expert who brings more than fifteen years of experience to the human services field as a grassroots advocate, professor and political consultant. Dr. Banks bravely tells her story as a triumphant survivor and lends her voice to the social justice and sustainability movement as a television host and motivational speaker. A dedicated entrepreneur and leadership expert, Dr. Banks is the President of The LeNetta Banks Group, LLC, a professional development training company.

As a former Air Force Captain, Ms. Banks was the first African-American from Rochester, NY to graduate from the U.S. Air Force Academy. She holds a B.S. in Behavioral Science-Psychology, M.S. in Human Services and Diversity Studies, and a PhD in Human Services from Capella University, researching domestic violence re-victimization.

What Does the Bible Really Say About Domestic Violence?

To the friends, family, co-workers, and community leaders of those dealing with domestic violence: I understand that you may have felt frustrated and powerless as you watched misery in motion from the sidelines. I get that you just wanted to keep your loved one safe and happy, but they kept returning to the scene of the crime. I know that you weren't sure what to say or even what not to say about domestic violence recovery, and I'm sorry for the pain that it caused you. I hope this letter brings you healing.

It's disappointing that with all the unspoken duties of a family member or friend, solving social ills may be added to your list. Certainly there are resources and experts on domestic violence, criminal justice, and mental health. But the truth is, friend, clergy member, co-worker, sister, we usually come to you first. And while I don't want you to play the hero and get entangled in my mess, I want you to know what to say to point me in the right direction. Domestic violence is a life or death issue, and as the old saying goes, "the time to learn CPR is not when someone is lying on the floor". Let this be a brief training manual to bring understanding, compassion, information and empowerment to all of us.

As a man or woman of God, I want you to be knowledgeable about this topic and up to speed on the current definitions, laws, and policies surrounding domestic violence. We need not be in the dark on this when the world is making all the decisions. We, as the body of Christ, can lead the charge.

"…for the children of this world are in their generation wiser than the children of light." Luke 16:8b

Also, men and women of God, be aware that this is first, a spiritual battle. And although you are a bystander, remember the warning found in 1 Corinthians 10:12: "Therefore let him that thinks he stands take heed lest he fall."

Let's start thinking differently about domestic violence, identify what it is, what the Bible says about it, and our response to it. Remember, it's not a fair fight, because in the end WE WIN!

CONTENTS

CHAPTER ONE: CAN WE LOOK AT DOMESTIC VIOLENCE DIFFERENTLY?

DOMESTIC violence is an ugly topic that many in or outside the church don't want to talk about or deal with. However, it's an epidemic that is tearing our communities apart. I believe that the church should lead the charge in order to take back our families by force!

...the kingdom of God suffers violence, and the violent, take it by force. - Matthew 11:12 NKJV

One of the tactics of the enemy is to wear out the saints (Daniel 7:25), and we've been tricked, lullabied into thinking that an abusive lifestyle is normal, traditional and even Biblical. But it does not line up with God's word, and I'm here to expose the enemy!

The thief does not come except to steal, and to kill, and to destroy. I have come that they may have life, and that they may have it more abundantly. - John 10:10 NKJV

One out of every four relationships suffers from domestic violence and more than half of the survivors will be victimized again.[1] Daily, one out of three women is murdered by her intimate partner, accounting for thirty percent of women's homicides.[2]

Because the statistics are so high, realize that there are many victims and survivors around you at all times. But there is hope. I'm a witness that you can come out of the fire and not smell like smoke (Daniel 3:27).

Often you, the friend, co-worker, family member, community leader, are the reason we stay or leave, live or die. It's that spiritual hand-to-hand combat where the real work is done.

LORD! Teach my hands to war and my fingers to fight! - Psalm 144:1

CHAPTER TWO: SO WHAT IS DOMESTIC VIOLENCE?

DOMESTIC Violence is not just about fighting. It's **about power and control.** So physical fighting like kicking, punching, slapping, shoving, intimidation, backing into corners, brandishing weapons—all are forms of gaining power and control.3

But power and control can also be gained without laying a hand on a person. Often, only the well-trained eye can see these other methods, but they are very effective.

Other Types of Abuse

Financial abuse: keeping finances secret, no access to money/information, causing one to lose a job or housing. Often the main reason why victims stay is because of finances3.

Verbal abuse: yelling, name-calling, putdowns, insults, cursing, negative comments about your beliefs, verbal argument until the victim surrenders his/her opinion, and forced conversations3.

Psychological/emotional abuse: any behavior that leads to psychological trauma. This behavior may include threatening mind games, humiliating, isolating, intimidating, ignoring, abandoning, and other controlling behavior3.

Abuse often happens gradually. It's almost unheard of for an abuser to go on a first date, slap their victim and convince them to stay in that relationship. No. It's gradual. As the old saying goes: If you tried to put a frog in boiling water, he would jump right out. But if you put him in cool water and then slowly turn up the heat, before the frog realizes it, he'll be cooked.

Verbal abuse, putdowns, isolation, stalking, 20-30 texts in an hour, intimidation, all eat away at your self-esteem and ability to think for yourself, trust, and make your own decisions. A victim may end up with Post Traumatic Stress Disorder symptoms. He or she may lose track of time, have poor memory, anxiety or depression. And soon the victim is a shell of the person you knew and loved[3].

Oh, so is it okay for a woman to hit a man?

NO! Ultimately domestic violence is about power and control, whether male or female. It is **not okay** for females to abuse either. No one gets a pass! Even self-defense can quickly turn into murder and the victim is imprisoned for life. Domestic violence is about who has the power, who owns the purse, the house, or has information he/she can hold over the victim.

If you are debating the point that a woman should not hit a man and provoke him, realize that you are already talking about an unhealthy relationship and a crime! Elevate your mind set to know the difference. We should be past the mindset that "if you fight like a man expect to get beat like a man" because **THERE SHOULD BE NO FIGHTING!** Men feel ashamed to report abuse just like women feel ashamed to report abuse. Contrary to popular belief, it does not feel socially acceptable for anyone to report abuse. But the real issue is the abuse, not who is wrong and "more wrong". There is no such thing as "more wrong" and no justification for domestic violence. It is wrong, sinful, and illegal. *Any other questions?*

Domestic Violence Is NOT simply poor anger management.

So now that we know what Domestic Violence is by definition, let's look at what it is not. Domestic Violence is not anger management or just "crazy" issues. If it was, the abusers would fight their bosses, friends, co-workers, and strangers. But no, they only abuse the ones they groom and feel they have control over[3].

CHAPTER THREE: WHAT DOES THE BIBLE SAY ABOUT DOMESTIC VIOLENCE?

DOMESTIC Violence is a sin and a crime! We are to obey the laws of the land (Romans 13:1-7).

In addition to the national and state laws against domestic violence, the federal Violence Against Women's Act (VAWA) of 1994 states that "a domestic violence misdemeanor is one in which someone is convicted for a crime committed by an intimate partner, parent, or guardian of the victim that required the use or attempted use of physical force or the threatened use of a deadly weapon" (Section 922 (g)[9]). VAWA also implements mandatory arrest or pro-arrest programs and policies in police departments, including protection order violations (Part U, SEC. 2101).

Beside the fact that domestic violence is illegal, it is also contrary to the word of God in every way.

Normally, when I speak on abuse I am asked about the role of submission in marriage. Someone usually exclaims Ephesians 5:24: *"So let the wives be (subject) to their own husbands in everything."* However, domestic violence is a perverted form of submission. So let's look deeper into the entire passage:

Ephesians 5:21 Submitting yourselves one to another in the fear of God.

Submitting yourselves "one to another" means that everyone has a role to play in submission. It is not just the duty of the wife, but the husband must also submit.

22 Wives, submit yourselves unto your own husbands, as unto the Lord.

Notice the Bible urges wives to complete a personal act and choose to "submit yourselves." No one is forcing the submission. It is a decision the wife makes even before the Bible dictates the husbands' duties.

23 For the husband is the head of the wife, even as Christ is the head of the church: and he is the saviour of the body.

24 Therefore as the church is subject unto Christ, so let the wives be to their own husbands in everything.

We understand that submission is a reaction to the leadership role of the husband. Similar to a well-run company, there are leadership positions and job descriptions. Let's look at the job description of the husband.

25 Husbands, love your wives, even as Christ also loved the church, and gave himself for it;

26 That he might sanctify and cleanse it with the washing of water by the word,

27 That he might present it to himself a glorious church, not having spot, or wrinkle, or any such thing; but that it should be holy and without blemish.

Interesting, the Bible does not say that in order to fulfill the leadership role, the husband must be a tyrant and lord. No. The Bible admonishes the husband to love, sanctify, and cleanse. These are the opposite of verbal, emotional, or physical abuse.

28 So ought men to love their wives as their own bodies. He that loveth his wife loveth himself.

This chapter goes further and explains exactly how a husband ought to love his wife. To love a person as you love yourself sounds simple enough, but again, the next verse takes the concept of love a step further and shares what love is not.

29 For no man ever yet hated his own flesh; but nourisheth and cherisheth it, even as the Lord the church.

The word says it is impossible to hate your own flesh! Instead, it is natural to nourish and cherish yourself. Therefore, one must love his or her spouse like Christ loves the church – nourish and cherish your spouse. Within the context of this scripture and throughout the Bible, there are kind words to describe love and marriage. You cannot justify abuse by manipulating the concept of submission. Some Christians love to throw the word "submission" around, but even God Himself doesn't force me to do anything. He gives me free will. That's what makes it a real relationship. Submission is my choice. If it isn't a choice, it's not a healthy relationship. It is slavery!

CHAPTER FOUR: WHAT WOULD JESUS SAY ABOUT DOMESTIC VIOLENCE?

MANY say that there is no specific reference from Jesus on the topic of domestic violence. However, Jesus had a habit of taking the law, raising the standard, and dealing with the heart. Take a look at what He said about adultery and lust:

You have heard that it was said, 'YOU SHALL NOT COMMIT ADULTERY'; 28 but I say to you that everyone who looks at a woman with lust for her has already committed adultery with her in his heart. - Matthew 5:27

In fact, earlier in this passage Jesus compares verbal abuse to murder:

Matthew 5:21 - *Ye have heard that it was said of them of old time, Thou shalt not kill; and whosoever shall kill shall be in danger of the judgment:*

22 But I say unto you, That whosoever is angry with his brother without a cause shall be in danger of the judgment: and whosoever shall say to his brother, Raca, shall be in danger of the council: but whosoever shall say, Thou fool, shall be in danger of hell fire."

If Jesus compares verbal putdowns as murder, how do you think He feels about physical abuse?

Even the fruit of domestic violence is anti-Christ at its core. Domestic violence in any form is the work of the enemy. *"The thief does not come except to steal, and to kill, and to destroy. I have come that they may have life, and that they may have it more abundantly."* – John 10:10.

Domestic violence always kills something. Abuse kills your destiny, your spirit, your self-worth, your joy, and sadly, it often kills the body. How can someone put you down and say God is behind it?

God said: you are *"...fearfully and wonderfully made..."* - Psalm 139:14. You are to be honored and treated delicately.

"Husbands, likewise, dwell with them with understanding, giving honor to the wife, as to the weaker vessel (glass, fine china), and as being heirs together of the grace of life, that your prayers may not be hindered." – 1 Peter 3:7

This does not mean women are weak. This is a metaphor for how one should treat his wife. The wife is to be given honor and treated as fine china. What do we do with fine china in our home? Do we treat it like cheap dishes, put it in the dishwasher, and throw it on the table?

No. We honor the fine china and expensive glasses by placing them in a beautiful cabinet, lifted high above our other common possessions. The scriptures have nothing but beautiful analogies and kind words to describe marriage.

How can a controlling, mean, and abusive marriage resemble the love of Christ toward the Church? Words like love, understanding, nourish, cherish, cleanse and present should describe a Godly marriage.

CHAPTER FIVE: IS IT ANY OF MY BUSINESS?

IT is your business. It is the business of us all.

When domestic violence shows up at your job or family home it quickly becomes your business. The bullet knows no name. It is our duty to speak up! It is our business.

Ezekiel 33:7-9 tells us you have a duty to warn, or the blood is on your hands:

7 "So you, son of man: I have made you a watchman for the house of Israel; therefore you shall hear a word from My mouth and warn them for Me. 8 When I say to the wicked, 'O wicked man, you shall surely die!' and you do not speak to warn the wicked from his way, that wicked man shall die in his iniquity; but his blood I will require at your hand. 9 Nevertheless if you warn the wicked to turn from his way, and he does not turn from his way, he shall die in his iniquity; but you have delivered your soul."

The duty to warn is heavy, but how do you apply this to your life? It is not your job to play the hero, jump in the middle of a fight, or make demands. But don't wait until it is too late, looking into the casket, wishing you could have done more or said something. With proper training and strategy you can be effective in stopping the spirit of murder in its tracks!

CHAPTER SIX: WHY DOES SHE STAY?

I know you've said and done everything you could have to be helpful, and she stayed or she went back. WHY LORD!?

Victims have many valid reasons for staying:

It is very dangerous, and leaving doesn't always make her feel safe. Most deaths occur when the victim is trying to leave or once she has left. Staying safe after leaving is a serious process.

She feels stupid. She is ashamed or feels guilty for even allowing herself to be there. Although the victim did nothing wrong and the abuser should be the one who's embarrassed, the victim often feels ashamed. So when she finally confides in you, she will likely be downplaying the abuse. In my case, it took a counsellor to say, "Oh you had a fight? What kind of fight? Did he hit you, shove you, back you into a corner or choke you? She helped me face the truth and deal with it, not downplay it.

She loves him. "He's not always like this." Everything else is good except for the abuse.

She thinks she can handle it. But self-defense can turn into homicide. That could put the victim in prison for life.

Some victims may worry about consequences concerning their children. "The children will not be safe when I leave. What about visitations? What if I lose custody? At least we are taken care of. They love their dad and this will hurt them more." These are all real concerns and there are no easy answers. When I learned that 90% of boys who witness domestic violence will repeat it, that helped me leave. I knew I could stop this generational curse.

We are not sure if leaving the abuser falls in line with our religious beliefs. Many of us have received religious counsel that told us to stay. Our clergy and family members may have been misinformed, and we have been taught that leaving is against God's will. So we need to know what God thinks about our situation before leaving. Share the Word of God. It has power!

Money, money, money! Honestly, the number one reason for staying or returning to abuse is because we cannot afford to leave or live independently...yet. Most likely, even if we are working, our finances have been tied up in such a way as to keep us from becoming independent. But it costs money to leave, move, find employment, take care of children, obtain legal help, time off of work, etc.

Simply taking extra measures to stay safe can be expensive. It may take a long time to get back on our feet, and staying with friends and family is not a long term solution. We often end up back in the hands of the abuser just so we can survive financially. There are other resources and options for a long term plan, but we need a great support system to be able to see that.

CHAPTER SEVEN: WHAT TO SAY - WHAT NOT TO SAY

FIRST let's discuss what NOT to say:

Don't blame the victim! You never really know who's a victim. Even when discussing with friends or your neighbor about the professional athletes in the news for domestic violence issues, don't call the victim stupid or say it's her fault for staying.

Don't ask what she did to "provoke" the abuse, or shame the victim in any way. Even when you're talking about strangers, I can identify with the victim. As my friend, I value your opinion, and your judgmental comments make it harder for me to come forward. Silently, I feel victimized again.

Don't Play the Hero. Don't demand that I leave with you right now! When I am in the middle of abuse, I may or may not even realize that I am being abused. It's as if I'm drowning, but you're not a trained life guard, yet you're trying to help me. So I may pull you in with me. Or, I may be trying to protect you from danger by not telling you what is really going on. I may be holding on to the one shred of dignity I have left by holding up my head and pressing through my situation.

But I am in desperate need of help. Instead of seeing me as a willing participant, see my relationship as a hostage situation. Would you handle a hostage situation by yourself, or would you let the professionals handle it? Trust me, I would leave if it was safe, but I know how crazy this person is, and I am terrified for a reason. Believe me.

Don't say what you wouldn't do. "I would never put up with that. I would kill him if he did that to me, etc." Millions of people go through domestic violence and most of them respond very similarly. So actually, if you were me, you'd probably do the same thing. Domestic abuse creates a cycle and a syndrome, so don't judge. I don't want you to ever have to find out "what you would do". Simply direct me to help, and encourage me along the way.

Most victims leave seven times before finally leaving for good4. To be successful, the victim has to have a short and long term plan.

Plans fail for lack of counsel but with many advisors they succeed. - Proverbs 15:22.

What should I say?

Build me up spiritually and emotionally. For years I may have been beaten down emotionally and led to believe that I couldn't make a decision or survive on my own. Remind me what the Bible says about me. Remind me that God loves me. That this is not His best for me. Faith comes by hearing, so share testimonies of how God delivers, heals, and overcomes.

Tell me I'm smart. Acknowledge the positive things I'm doing in my life and for my family.

Encourage me to go achieve my goals. This will help me re-build self-esteem, self-efficacy, and self-worth.

Find ways to help me build financially. Going back to school, learning employment skills, exploring entrepreneurial avenues, and other ways to keep me financially independent can help me make a better decision, not one based on financial desperation.

Ask me: "How can I help you?" You may not be the expert, but you can learn about your local resources. Help build a support system for me and my family.

Remind me that I am not alone. One out of three women and one out of four men experience some form of domestic violence5. Unfortunately, the numbers are very high, but remind me that I was strong enough to want to change.

Tell me I can do this. Remind me that it may be difficult at first, but I can overcome this. Remind me that I've been strong, not weak, to even endure this far. Show me examples of other powerhouse women who have survived and thrived.

Chapter Eight: Is It Okay to Leave?

FRIEND, it's not just a matter of asking, "Can I leave abuse?" I'm not even sure if it's okay to leave.

David fled! (1 Samuel 19)

David and Saul are a biblical example of the cycle of abuse. This proves that abuse can happen in all types of relationships besides marriage.

The enemy is trying to kill you. And even though the person who is letting the devil use them is sorry and vows not to do it again, without professional help, he/she will.

I decided to say to my abuser, "When you relapse I will not be there!" Because that could mean my life.

Does Forgiveness Mean I Should Go Back?

I hear often, "I am staying and just waiting for God to fix him…I am praying for him, that he will change and the abuse will stop." My response is that you, the survivor, are doing all the work, counseling, rebuilding. But where are the abuser's faith AND works?

The facts are that re-victimization rates are very high. Over 75% of victims are victimized again[1].

The work to learn how to have a healthy relationship after professional help is extremely difficult, especially when the abuser first has to be convinced that he or she has a problem. The need for spiritual deliverance from generational curses, generational training, and familiar spirits is crucial at this point. **The victim cannot lead the charge on the abuser's change.**

"But someone will say, "You have faith, and I have works." Show me your faith without your works, and I will show you my faith by my works." – James 2:18

Don't use prayer as a form of manipulation where YOU are trying to change someone. Do you know how hard it is to change yourself? Even when you want to change, it is very difficult. So how is it that YOU will change someone else?

Get out and stay safe

Proverbs 22:3 & 27:12 – *"A prudent man foresees evil and hides himself, But the simple pass on and are punished."*

Friend, don't use this verse to call me stupid. Just pray it over me and remind me that I should use wisdom as I seek safety.

Friend, keep me focused on the spiritual battle and remind me that retaliation is not necessary.

David had the opportunity to retaliate, but he recognized that God is the judge, not him. It is possible to forgive and remain safe by leaving a dangerous situation. The abuser is not the enemy.

"We wrestle not against flesh and blood…" – Ephesians 6:12.

Even David, when he had a chance to kill Saul, remembered, *"Touch not mine anointed ones and do my prophet no harm."* - 1 Samuel 24:6. Forgiveness frees us spiritually and allows us to move forward, focused on God's will.

Remind me that the abuser is not my enemy. God has my back, but faith requires action (James 2:17).

CHAPTER NINE: DIVORCE IN RESPONSE TO ABUSE?

MALACHI 2:16 – *"I hate divorce, says the Lord God of Israel,.."* We pull this verse out like a weapon to say why an abused women should stay in a relationship. I've even heard of ministers who say, "Well, Jesus was abused so you can be too."

The devil is a liar! Jesus was already wounded for my transgressions, already bruised for my iniquities! (Isaiah 53:5) It was finished at the cross! I am not to be abused. Yes, God hates divorce and He hates murder too!

So let's read Malachi 2:15-16 in context.

"…Therefore take heed to your spirit, And let none deal treacherously with the wife of his youth.16 "For the Lord God of Israel says that He hates divorce, For it covers one's garment with violence…"

Tell me: "Friend, whether or not you believe a divorce or re-marriage is an appropriate option is not our main concern right now. I just want you to be alive to make that decision."

I recognize that there are different denominational belief systems surrounding divorce. However, do not allow a theological loophole to justify abuse.

Friend, just help me to stay alive to make the choice.

Chapter Ten: Thank You, Friend

THERE is so much I want to say about domestic abuse, but more importantly, I want to explain how vital your friendship is to me.

I know it had to hurt watching me go through so much pain, abuse, fear, and abandonment. I'm sure it had to be frustrating to hear my highs and lows over the phone as the cycle of abuse continued.

It has taken years to recover and you've been there through them all.

Friend, you are not an innocent bystander. You are part of the solution. You have the word of God to apply practically to our lives to keep us focused on God's will for our lives.

So what's next?

Let's learn about what a healthy relationship is. What is the right way to argue? Let's meet healthy examples and mentors of Godly relationships and rebuild our community. There is so much hope for a great future and great relationships!

"He that began a good work in you will perform it until the day of Jesus Christ." - Philippians 1:6.

Isaiah 54

A Perpetual Covenant of Peace

TO THE SINGLE WOMEN:

"Sing, O barren,
You who have not borne!
Break forth into singing, and cry aloud,
You who have not laboured with child!
For more are the children of the desolate

Than the children of the married woman," says the Lord.
2 "Enlarge the place of your tent,
And let them stretch out the curtains of your dwellings;
Do not spare;
Lengthen your cords,
And strengthen your stakes.
3 For you shall expand to the right and to the left,
And your descendants will inherit the nations,
And make the desolate cities inhabited."

DIVORCED? SINGLE AGAIN? ABANDONED?

4 "Do not fear, for you will not be ashamed;
Neither be disgraced, for you will not be put to shame;
For you will forget the shame of your youth,
And will not remember the reproach of your widowhood anymore.
5 For your Maker is your husband,
The Lord of hosts is His name;
And your Redeemer is the Holy One of Israel;
He is called the God of the whole earth.
6 For the Lord has called you
Like a woman forsaken and grieved in spirit,
Like a youthful wife when you were refused,"
Says your God.

WHAT ABOUT MY CHILDREN?

"All your children shall be taught by the Lord,
And great shall be the peace of your children.
14 In righteousness you shall be established;
You shall be far from oppression, for you shall not fear;
And from terror, for it shall not come near you.
Indeed they shall surely assemble, but not because of Me.
Whoever assembles against you shall fall for your sake."

JUST SO WE ARE CLEAR, GOD PROMISES:

17 No weapon formed against you shall prosper, And every tongue which rises against you in judgment You shall condemn. This is the heritage of the servants of the Lord, And their righteousness is from Me," Says the Lord.

AMEN! AMEN! AMEN!

NOTES:

Kuijpers et al, K. F., van der Knaap, L. M., & Winkel, F. W. (2012). Risk of re-victimization of intimate partner violence: The role of attachment, anger and violent behavior of the victim. Journal of family violence, 27(1), 33-44.

Sulak, T. N., Saxon, T. F., & Fearon, D. (2014). Applying the Theory of Reasoned Action to Domestic Violence Reporting Behavior: The Role of Sex and Victimization. Journal of Family Violence, 29(2), 165-173.

World Health Organization. (2014). Violence against women: intimate partner and sexual violence against women: intimate partner and sexual violence have serious short and long-term physical, mental and sexual and reproductive health problems for survivors: fact sheet.

2 Bureau of Justice Statistics. (2006). Intimate partner violence in the U.S. 1993-2004. Washington, DC: Bureau of Justice Statistics, U. S. Department of Justice.

Rennison, C. M. (2003). Intimate partner violence, 1993-2001. Washington, DC: Bureau of Justice Statistics, U. S. Department of Justice. World Health Organization. (2013). Policy and clinical practice guidelines for responding to intimate partner violence and sexual violence. Geneva, Switzerland, Author.

3 National Coalition Against Domestic Violence (2014). Need support. Retrieved on May 21, 2014 from www.ncadv.org/need-support/what-is-domestic-violence.

4 Crosbie-Burnett, M., & Giles-Sims, J. (1991). Marital power in stepfather families: A test of normative-resource theory. Journal of Family Psychology, 4(4), 484.

5 Black, M. C., Basile, K. C., Breiding, M. J., Smith, S. G., Walters, M. L.,Merrick, M. T., & Stevens, M. R. (2011). National intimate partner and sexual violence survey. Atlanta, GA: Centers for Disease Control and Prevention.

6 Civic Impulse. (2015). S. 47 — 113th Congress: Violence Against Women Reauthorization Act of 2013.

Retrieved from: www.govtrack.us/congress/bills/113/s47.

YOUR NOTES

YOUR NOTES

YOUR NOTES

www.ingramcontent.com/pod-product-compliance
Lightning Source LLC
Chambersburg PA
CBHW062029280526
45787CB00005B/2259